PRAISE FOR
FRED KOREMATSU SPEAKS UP:

Winner, Carter G. Woodson Book Award
Winner, New-York Historical Society Children's Book Prize
A *Kirkus* Best Book of the Year
Honor Title, Jane Addams Children's Book Award
Finalist, Cybils Awards
Nominee, Georgia Book Award
Featured on National Public Radio
An ACL Outstanding Title

"Atkins and Yogi raise good questions...that will inspire a new generation of activists. This first book in the Fighting for Justice series is a must-read for all civics classrooms."—*Kirkus Reviews* (starred review)

"An invaluable profile of a civil rights hero whose story deserves greater attention. Middle schoolers will take to the superb writing and original format."—Laura Simeon, *School Library Journal* (starred review)

"Its appeal and user-friendly presentation are undeniable."—*Booklist*

"A new book about civil rights icon Fred Korematsu's fight against Japanese American incarceration wants to teach young readers to 'stand up for what is right.'"—Frances Kai-Hwa Wang, *NBC News*

"A tutorial on civil rights, an introductory civics lesson, and a clarion call to action."—Susan Faust, *San Francisco Chronicle*

"The relevance of the themes in *Fred Korematsu Speaks Up* in today's world is unmistakable."—Eileen Kurahashi, *Los Angeles Review of Books*

"This story should be in every classroom."—*Rethinking Schools*

"Easily one of the best nonfiction children's books on any aspect of Asian American history."—Brian Niiya, content editor for Densho

FRED KOREMATSU
SPEAKS UP

Laura Atkins and Stan Yogi

Illustrated by Yutaka Houlette

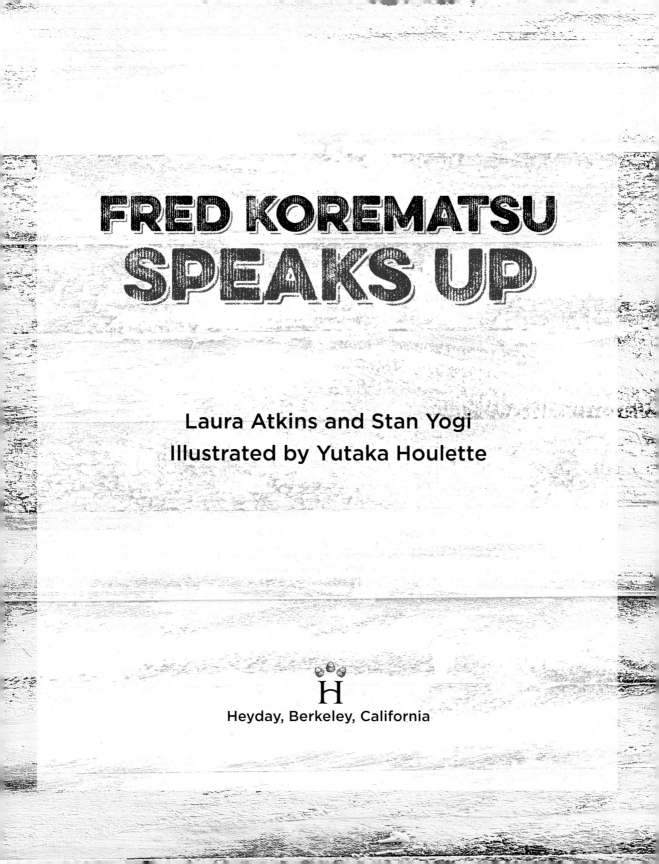

Heyday, Berkeley, California

HAVE YOU EVER SPOKEN UP WHEN YOU SAW SOMETHING THAT WASN'T RIGHT?

Sometimes people treat one another badly. Sometimes rules and laws are unfair. It can take one brave person, or a group of people acting together, to speak up and make a difference.

Throughout history, people have fought for justice, even when it meant taking a stand against powerful people or working hard to make their voices heard.

In the end, these people helped to make the world a fairer place.

Fred Korematsu spoke up for justice.

You can speak up for justice too.

Support for this printing was provided by the California State Library's California Civil Liberties Public Education Program.

In this book, italics are used to denote direct quotes, whether speech or thoughts. Corresponding sources appear on page 92.

Library of Congress Cataloging-in-Publication Data

Names: Atkins, Laura, author. | Yogi, Stan, author.
Title: Fred Korematsu speaks up / by Laura Atkins and Stan Yogi ;
    illustrations by Yutaka Houlette.
Description: Berkeley, California : Heyday, [2016] | Series: Fighting for
    justice | Includes bibliographical references and index.
Identifiers: LCCN 2016008098 | ISBN 9781597143684 (hardcover : alk. paper)
Subjects: LCSH: Korematsu, Fred, 1919-2005--Trials, litigation,
    etc.--Juvenile literature. | Japanese Americans--Evacuation and
    relocation, 1942-1945--Juvenile literature. | Japanese Americans--Civil
    rights--History--20th century--Juvenile literature.
Classification: LCC KF228.K59 A85 2016 | DDC 341.6/7--dc23
LC record available at http://lccn.loc.gov/2016008098

Cover Illustration: Yutaka Houlette

Back Cover Photographs (from left to right): by Dorothea Lange, courtesy of the National Archives and Records Administration; courtesy of Karen Korematsu at the Fred T. Korematsu Institute; by Dorothea Lange, courtesy of the National Archives and Records Administration

Cover Design: Ashley Ingram

Interior Design/Typesetting: Nancy Austin

See Image and Text Credits and Permissions on page 95.

Orders, inquiries, and correspondence should be addressed to:
    Heyday
    P.O. Box 9145, Berkeley, CA 94709
    (510) 549-3564, Fax (510) 549-1889
    www.heydaybooks.com

Printed in China by Printplus Limited
10 9 8 7 6 5

CONTENTS

1.
GETTING
A HAIRCUT

Fred's hair needs cutting.
His friends have the snazziest styles—
short and sharp,
slicked down and combed back.
All the rage.

Up until now, Fred's mother
has cut his hair.
Straight.
Simple.
Fred wants to get his hair cut
by a real barber.

He walks into his local barbershop.
The waxy smell of pomade oil
mingles with the sound of snipping scissors.

Hey boy, what do you want?
the barber says.

I just want to get a haircut,
Fred tells him.

We don't cut hair of your kind.

Why?
Because Fred's parents are from Japan.
The barbershop won't serve people
who look like Fred.

Fred knows
this isn't fair.
He has as much right to that
haircut as any of his friends.

Fred walks out
past other barbershops
that will not cut his hair
and restaurants
that will not serve him food.

He goes to Oakland's Chinatown
where people who look like Fred
are welcome.

He gets his hair cut
in the latest style
just like his friends.

DISCRIMINATION

Fred grew up in Oakland, California. When the barber refused to cut Fred's hair, he discriminated against Fred because of how he looked. He treated Fred differently from White customers because Fred wasn't White like the barber. He was Japanese American.

Throughout United States history, many different groups have experienced this kind of discrimination and worse.

People experience discrimination because of their ancestry—because they or their parents come from another country. People of color also face discrimination because of their race. Fred faced discrimination for both of these reasons.

Fred in the year 1940.

JAPANESE AMERICAN: an American of Japanese ancestry.

DISCRIMINATION: the act of treating a person or group unfairly because of what they look like or what they believe. Discrimination based on race is called racism.

ANCESTRY: a person's family origin or background.

RACE: a group of people identified as similar to one another because of supposed physical traits, such as skin color.

HAVE YOU EVER BEEN TREATED BADLY BECAUSE OF HOW YOU LOOK OR SPEAK?

In the 1840s and 1850s, immigrants from Ireland faced discrimination from Americans in East Coast cities who considered the Irish violent and dangerous. Cartoons like this supported these stereotypes.

THE IRISH FRANKENSTEIN.

IMMIGRANT: someone who moves to a new country to live there permanently.

STEREOTYPE: an unfair and untrue belief about a group of people that lumps all of them together as being the same, instead of unique individuals.

PACIFIC CHIVALRY.
Encouragement to Chinese Immigration.

This 1869 cartoon of a White man attacking a Chinese immigrant shows the anger many Americans felt toward Chinese people. In the late 1800s, many Chinese came to the Western United States to mine for gold and build railroads.

TIMELINE

1865
Civil War ends. Slavery is abolished, but Southern states begin passing segregation laws.

1882
United States stops allowing Chinese laborers into the country. This was called the Chinese Exclusion Act.

1896
United States Supreme Court decides segregation is legal.

4

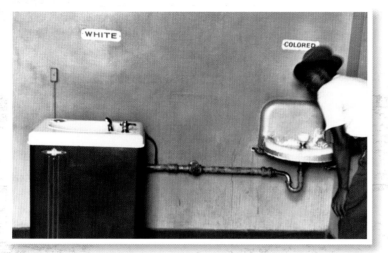

For more than one hundred years, African Americans living in many parts of the United States could not use the same drinking fountains as White people. They could not go to the same schools, shop in the same stores, or eat in the same restaurants. Even bathrooms were segregated.

This sign at a Texas business showed that Mexican and Spanish-speaking people were not welcome. Mexican immigrants and their children in Southwestern states often faced the same kinds of segregation as African Americans.

WHY DO YOU THINK DISCRIMINATION HAPPENS?

1932
United States government begins to force Mexican immigrants and Mexican Americans to leave the country.

1943
United States allows Chinese laborers into the country.

1954
United States Supreme Court decides segregation is illegal.

2.
PRUNING ROSES

Fred's father and mother,
Kakusaburo and Kotsui,
moved to the United States
from faraway Japan
in the early 1900s
looking for new opportunities.

They have four sons.
Born in 1919, Fred comes third.
His parents name him Toyosaburo.

His first-grade teacher
can't get her tongue around
the Japanese sounds.

How would you like to be called Fred?
she asks.

He takes to this new name,
and it sticks.

Everyone in Fred's family works hard
at the flower nursery,
which they own,
paid for through
hours
and years
of waking early
to prune roses
and tend carnations.
They sell their blossoms
to local flower shops.

Chores for Fred and his brothers
keep them working
all the time.

Fred's oldest brother, Hi,
is the favorite.
Harry, the second, is smart.
Baby brother Joe is cute.

Fred doesn't fit.
He wants to go his own way
and dreams of a future
that does not include
the flower nursery.

Fred's parents love Japan,
country of their childhood.

They take Fred and his brothers
to the drafty auditorium
of the Buddhist temple

to see black-and-white movies
about fierce samurai warriors
fighting with long swords.

They celebrate Boy's Day
on May fifth of each year,
flying colorful streamers
in the shape of koi fish.
One for each son.

Fred's parents speak Japanese at home
and want their boys to do the same.
They bring in a tutor.

But Japanese isn't Fred's language.
He speaks English.

What is Japan to him?
So far away.
A land he has never seen.

Fred—he is an American.

Baby Fred and his mother.

DISCRIMINATION AGAINST JAPANESE AMERICANS

ISSEI:
the Japanese word for "first generation," used to describe people who permanently moved from Japan to the United States.

NISEI:
the Japanese word for "second generation," used to describe children born to the Issei in the United States.

CULTURE:
knowledge, beliefs, and behavior that people learn and pass on to future generations.

When Fred's parents arrived in California in the early 1900s, many Americans were angry that Japanese people were moving to the United States. They did not like that Japanese immigrants (known as the Issei) were different. They were not White. They spoke Japanese, not English. They ate rice, not potatoes.

The children of the Issei (known as the Nisei) learned the Japanese customs and traditions of their parents. They also learned English and connected with American culture through movies, music, and sports. Issei parents were often upset when their Nisei children were not interested in Japanese culture, like Fred's parents were when he didn't want to learn Japanese.

Fred and his family in their flower nursery. From left to right: Fred's father, Kakusaburo; Fred's mother, Kotsui; Fred; Fred's brothers Joe, Harry, and Hi. In 1913, Fred's father bought twenty-five acres of land in Oakland for the family's home and nursery, just before California stopped allowing Japanese immigrants to own land.

HAVE YOU OR OTHERS IN YOUR FAMILY FACED DISCRIMINATION FOR COMING FROM A DIFFERENT COUNTRY?

Many White people, like this woman, wanted all Japanese—Issei and Nisei—out of their neighborhoods, out of their schools, and out of their country. The word *Jap* used in this sign is a racist name for Japanese people. In 1924, government leaders changed the law and decided that no more Japanese could move to the United States.

GOVERNMENT:
a system of rules that controls a community of people. Government can also mean the people in charge of making those rules.

LAW:
a rule that the government makes.

This painting by Japanese American artist Henry Sugimoto shows a family feeling discouraged by a hateful sign. Many White farmers believed that the Issei were taking their jobs. In reality, Japanese immigrant farmers often took over unwanted, abandoned property, and transformed the land into productive farms.

TIMELINE

1905
Fred's father moves to the United States.

1913
The State of California passes the Alien Land Law, making it illegal for Issei to own land.

1914
Fred's mother moves to the United States and marries Fred's father.

1919
January 30
Fred is born.

1924
United States stops allowing Japanese immigrants into the country.

3.
BEING A TEEN

Fred finds his home
at school
and with his friends.

He hangs around with his buddy Walt
from Boy Scout Troop 8.
Together they camp and goof off
in the Oakland Hills.

Fred's parents say that
he gets into mischief,
like when he and Walt sneak oranges
from a neighbor's tree,
or when they are twelve years old
and hop in the car—
Walt too young to drive—
to swim at the Plunge.

In high school Fred
runs track and plays tennis.

The ball zooms
back and forth,
served and returned.

Each school day starts with a
pledge to the United States.
Fred learns about the Constitution,
which states that all Americans
are free and have equal rights.

Fred feels this freedom and equality at school.

But outside, many people
stare
because of his Japanese face.

These days Japan is in the newspapers
for fighting with other countries.
The stares are growing meaner.

Fred doesn't talk a lot,
but he's not shy.
Especially when he does what he loves.

He is keen on the big band tunes
of Benny Goodman,
swings to the grooves of Duke Ellington
and jitterbugs at all the dances.

Tennis, Boy Scouts, homework.
Girls.

Fred hardly finds the nerve
to ask them out,
but he has crushes.

Just like any other boy
at any other high school.

Fred's Castlemont High yearbook, 1937.

BEING AN AMERICAN CITIZEN

When Fred was growing up in the 1920s and 1930s, the United States government would not allow Issei, like his parents, to become American citizens because they had come from Japan. But White immigrants from Europe could become citizens.

Fred and his brothers were American citizens because they were born in the United States. But since Fred was Japanese American, other people didn't always see him as a citizen, or treat him like one.

The Empire of Japan had invaded China in 1931, and many Americans thought that the United States might go to war. They did not see the difference between Americans of Japanese ancestry, like Fred, and citizens of the Japanese Empire.

Who Is an American?

The Constitution says that anyone born in the United States is an American citizen. But a young Chinese American cook named Wong Kim Ark had to fight for this right.

Wong Kim Ark was born in San Francisco in 1873. He took a trip to China to visit his family when he was twenty-two. But when Wong returned home by ship to San Francisco, an official at the port would not allow him back into the country. The official claimed that Wong was not an American citizen because his Chinese immigrant parents were not allowed to become citizens.

Wong fought this official in court. Eventually, his case went to the United States Supreme Court. The judges agreed with Wong that everyone born in the United States is a citizen. Wong's case helped others whose American citizenship was questioned because of their race and ancestry. Wong had fought for justice and won.

Wong Kim Ark.

Many immigrants from Europe who were White saw the Statue of Liberty in New York Harbor as they entered the country. They could become American citizens.

WHAT DOES IT MEAN TO YOU TO BE AN AMERICAN?

But Asian immigrants who arrived in the United States on the Pacific coast, like these women and children from China, could not become citizens because they were not White.

The United States Constitution is a document that outlines the system of beliefs and laws that govern the country. It was first written in 1789 and has been changed, or amended, twenty-seven times since. The Constitution lists the rights and freedoms that all American citizens have, such as the right to vote, the right to be treated fairly, and the right to speak freely. But sometimes these rights have been denied to people because of their race, ancestry, or for other reasons.

We the People

Article 1

RIGHT:
the freedom that people have to be, do, or have something.

TIMELINE

1789
United States Constitution is first written.

1898
Wong Kim Ark wins his case.

1937
Fred graduates from high school.

1952
Japanese immigrants are finally allowed to become United States citizens.

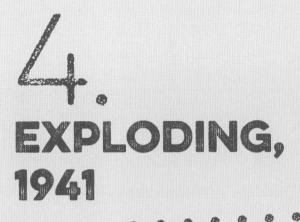

4.
EXPLODING, 1941

At twenty-two Fred is in love
with his dreamboat Ida,
daughter of Italian immigrants.

Their families
disapprove
because Fred is Japanese American
and Ida is Italian American.

But Fred loves Ida
and Ida loves Fred.
So they date
in secret.

There are rumblings in the world—
war is spreading.
The United States hasn't entered yet,
but the country is preparing
for the possibility.

Fred tries to join the military
to help fight for his country,
but he is rejected.

So Fred looks for another way
to support the United States.
He finds a job as a welder,
melting metal to build ships.

He saves his wages
to buy a Pontiac car,
a swanky ride for him and Ida.

Fred is good at the work.
His slim body slips into small spaces,
squeezing between the double bottoms of boats.
But he gets fired from his job
for being Japanese American.

Fear is building.

Ugly words—Japs go home, No room for Japs—
are smeared on shops and houses.
Hatred for anyone who looks
like Fred.

Fred asks Ida to marry him,
and she says yes.

His dreams spread out
in front of him.
Marriage.
A family.

December 7, 1941.
A bright Sunday morning.
The sun shines
on Fred and Ida
parked in the Oakland hills.

They read comics in the newspaper
and listen to songs on the radio.

Then the music stops.
A voice cuts in.

Bombs have rained down
on the navy base called
Pearl Harbor in Hawai'i.
Japanese pilots have killed
American soldiers.

Fred's stomach goes tight.
He has worried that the Empire of Japan
would do something crazy like this.

He drops Ida off and rushes home
to find his family huddled around the radio.
His mother is in tears.

Within hours
President Roosevelt declares
all Japanese immigrants
over fourteen years old
"alien enemies."

What will happen now?

Above: A ship called the USS *Arizona* burns in Pearl Harbor.

Below: United States Navy sailors look on as warplanes burn. Photographs like these shocked and frightened Americans, who wondered if the Empire of Japan would attack their cities and neighborhoods.

WARTIME PANIC AND DISCRIMINATION

On the early morning of Sunday, December 7, 1941, military warplanes from the Empire of Japan dropped bombs on the United States Navy base at Pearl Harbor in Hawai'i. More than 2,000 Americans died. Bombs damaged or destroyed 21 United States warships and 323 warplanes.

When Japanese Americans learned about the bombing of Pearl Harbor, they were shocked like other Americans. But they were also nervous about what would happen to them. They feared that the United States government would not trust them because of their Japanese ancestry.

And they were right. Hours after the bombs exploded, government officials arrested leaders in Japanese American communities—priests at Buddhist temples, editors of newspapers, presidents of clubs—even though they had done nothing wrong.

MILITARY:
the armed forces of a country, such as the army, navy, and coast guard, or members of those forces.

LOYAL:
being faithful and supportive. Disloyal: failing to be loyal.

HAVE YOU EVER BEEN BLAMED FOR SOMETHING JUST BECAUSE OF HOW YOU LOOK?

After the bombing of Pearl Harbor, the United States declared war on the Empire of Japan and entered the global conflict known as World War II. The Empire of Japan had sided with Germany and Italy, and the United States was now sided with China, France, the Soviet Union, and the United Kingdom.

The Japanese American owner of this store in Oakland hung the "I Am an American" sign the day after Pearl Harbor was bombed. He wanted to show that he was loyal to the United States, not to the Japanese Empire.

Hatred and discrimination against Issei and Nisei grew because they looked like the enemy. It did not make a difference that Nisei were American citizens, born and educated in the United States.

In this painting, artist Henry Sugimoto shows a government agent taking an Issei man away from his family's farm. Agents arrested thousands of Issei men because the government feared they might be spies. Their families had no idea where they were jailed. Many of the arrested men did not see their families for months.

SPIES: people who try secretly to get information about a country or organization.

ILLEGAL: against the law. Legal: allowed by law.

Love and the Law

At the time Fred and Ida were dating, it was unusual for people of different races to date. In California and most states, it was illegal for a White person to marry someone of a different race.

In 1909, Gunjiro Aoki (right), an Issei, wanted to marry his White girlfriend, Helen Gladys Emery (left). When Gunjiro visited Helen at her home in Corte Madera, California, a mob of angry White people threw bricks and shouted that they would cover him with tar and feathers. The couple had to go to Washington to get married. Many years later, Gunjiro's great-niece Brenda Wong Aoki uncovered their story and wrote a play about it. People of different races could not legally marry across the United States until 1967.

TIMELINE

1937
Empire of Japan invades China.

1940
Fred tries to join the military.

1941 December 7
Empire of Japan attacks Pearl Harbor in Hawai'i.

December 8
United States declares war on Empire of Japan.

1967
United States Supreme Court rules that people of different races can legally marry.

5.
DECIDING TO DEFY

Police raid the Korematsu home
taking flashlights, cameras—
anything they say can be used
to send signals to the enemy.

The people at the factory next door
install a bright spotlight
and shine it on Fred
when he stands in front of his house.
They think he and his family are spies
because they look like the people
who bombed their country.

My country too, Fred thinks.

Then President Franklin D. Roosevelt
signs an order allowing the military
to force all Japanese immigrants
and Japanese Americans
on the West Coast
from their homes.

Soon they will have to move to
what the government calls
"Assembly Centers."

Really prisons.

It is unclear when this
forced removal
will take place.
Just that it will be soon.

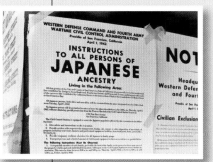

The government put
up posters like these in
West Coast areas where
Japanese Americans
lived, ordering all people
of Japanese ancestry
to report to be sent to
prison camps.

Fred feels the chaos
like a tornado
tearing up houses.

His parents scramble.
What will happen to their nursery?
They have to figure out what to bring—
only allowed what they can carry
in their hands.

All Fred can think about
is staying with Ida.
He comes up with a plan.
They will move away from the West Coast
to a state where Japanese Americans
can still be free.

He tells his parents
that he wants to leave California
rather than report to the prison camp.

You're old enough to know what to do, his parents say.
No time to think about his problems.
Go ahead.

Fred rents a room at a boarding house
until Ida is ready to move away with him.

He doesn't feel like a criminal
for disobeying the government's orders.
He knows he is a citizen
and should have the same rights
as any American.

But to get those rights
he has to pretend to be
someone else.

Fred changes his name to Clyde Sarah
and says he is Spanish Hawaiian.
He is able to hide in front of everyone
because people can't always tell
someone is Japanese American.

He feels strangely free—
living on his own, dating Ida,
riding on buses, going to movies.

But this feeling shatters
when he looks at newspapers.
Headlines scream: *Jap this and Jap that*.
He will not buy those ugly words.

Then one day
Fred sees pictures
in the newspaper
of Japanese Americans
marched into prison camps.

He thinks about his parents,
his brothers,
stuck
inside.

May 30, 1942.
Fred is walking down the street
when a police car drives up.
A policeman climbs out.
He wants to know who Fred is.

Fred tells the officer his made-up name,
hoping he will believe it.

Then an army jeep pulls over.
More policemen talk.

Fred waits.

And then they arrest him,
sweeping his freedom away.

FORCED REMOVAL AND IMPRISONMENT

Government agents searched the homes of Japanese American families like Fred's for evidence that they might be disloyal. The Constitution states that police officers cannot search people's homes without a good reason to suspect they have committed a crime. But government officials searched Fred's home even though there was no cause to think anyone in Fred's family had done anything wrong.

President Franklin D. Roosevelt signed Executive Order 9066 on February 19, 1942. This allowed military leaders to force Japanese Americans to move. Soon afterward, Lieutenant General John L. DeWitt, the military commander in charge of the Western states, ordered all Japanese Americans off the West Coast. He thought they could be spies. They would have to go to prison camps.

President Franklin D. Roosevelt.

The Constitution says that citizens have the right to a fair trial if they are accused of breaking the law. But General DeWitt's orders did not give Japanese Americans the chance to have trials to prove that they were not spies.

> EVIDENCE:
> a visible sign of having done something.
>
> EXECUTIVE ORDER:
> an order given by a president to government officials.

HAVE YOU EVER BEEN PUNISHED FOR SOMETHING YOU DIDN'T DO?

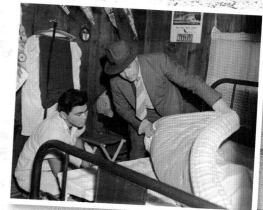
Government agents searched homes for items they thought could be used to send signals to ships or planes, and anything that might link a family to the Empire of Japan.

Fred's family had to figure out what to do with their nursery and home. Eventually, they found renters. After the government gave them formal orders to move, they had just days to decide what to take with them.

The government allowed Japanese Americans to take to the prison camps only one or two suitcases per person. So they had to decide quickly what to do with their belongings. Sometimes, friends and neighbors took care of Japanese Americans' property. But others took advantage of Japanese Americans, buying for little money the possessions they could not take with them.

Very few people spoke up to say that the government was violating Japanese Americans' rights.

An armed guard stands next to a bus that will take Japanese Americans to the prison camp where Fred's family was sent.

21538

The government assigned each Japanese American family a number. Everyone had to attach tags with the number to themselves and their belongings, like this girl has on her jacket. The Korematsu family number was 21538.

This painting by Henry Sugimoto, called *Junkshop Man Took Away Our Icebox,* shows a man taking away a family's refrigerator prior to them going to prison camp.

The Power of Pictures

The United States government created posters and pamphlets portraying Japanese as evil and dangerous. Newspapers and magazines were also filled with these kinds of pictures. Many people who saw these pictures again and again grew to fear Japanese and Japanese American people.

THIS IS THE ENEMY

The scary figure with the knife is wearing a hat with the Empire of Japan's flag.

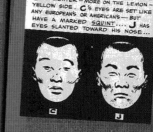

China was fighting on the same side as the United States during World War II. The United States Army created and distributed this pamphlet with instructions on how to tell apart people of Chinese and Japanese ancestry. Their goal was to uncover Japanese Americans in hiding, like Fred. Pictures like these also supported racial stereotypes.

TIMELINE – 1942

February 19
President Franklin D. Roosevelt signs Executive Order 9066.

March 24
Lieutenant General John L. DeWitt begins issuing orders forcing Japanese Americans from their homes into prison camps.

March
Fred decides not to go to prison camp and moves to a boarding house.

May 8
Fred's parents and brothers are forced to move to a prison camp.

May 30
Fred is arrested.

6.
SAYING YES

Jail becomes Fred's new home.
He sleeps on a hard bed
trapped behind bars.

Fred thinks that
Ida must be worried.
He didn't have a chance to talk to her
when he got caught.

One day a guard says,
You got a visitor.

Fred is taken to a meeting room.
A young man in a gray suit
shakes Fred's hand and introduces himself
as Ernest Besig, a lawyer.

I would like to help you, he says.

Fred can't afford a lawyer.
But Ernest says he will not charge any money.

He works for the American Civil Liberties Union
and read about Fred in the newspapers.
He hopes that Fred will fight the case against him,
which will also mean challenging the imprisonment of
all Japanese Americans as unconstitutional.

Ernest tells Fred that the fight could take a long time
with little chance of winning because
there is so much discrimination against
people who look like Fred.

Is he willing?

Fred thinks about it.
He doesn't want to go to the prison camp.
But more than that, he knows
that what the government is doing
is not fair.

He decides to fight.

Fred says
yes.

We'll fight it together,
Ernest says.
All the way.

Days later, Fred and Ernest go to the courthouse
to appear before a judge.
The judge says that Fred
is accused of breaking the law
by refusing to go
to the prison camp.

There will be an official legal case
against him.

If Fred can pay $2500,
more than the cost of three Pontiac cars,
he can leave jail to wait
for the next step in his case.

Fred doesn't have that kind of money.
But on the spot Ernest pays.
Fred can't believe it.
So much help from this man
he barely knows.

Fred sees that everyone in the United States
does not support what the government
is doing.

Ernest and Fred walk out together,
shoes click-clacking on the tile floors.
They open the heavy courthouse doors
into a blaze of sunlight.

Fred feels free again.

Then his eyes adjust to the brightness,
and he sees military police officers waiting for him.

They order Fred to get into their car
and
drive
away.

ALLIES IN COURT AND BEYOND

Ernest Besig was a lawyer who worked for the American Civil Liberties Union (ACLU), an organization that fights in court for

people's rights. From its beginning in 1920, the ACLU has fought against discrimination.

Ernest believed that it was wrong to put innocent Japanese Americans like Fred and his family in prison camps, and he wanted to help. He was an ally to Japanese Americans during a time when many other Americans feared and hated them.

Ernest Besig.

Ernest had been searching for a brave Japanese American who would fight the government's orders to report to prison camp. Through Fred's case, Ernest hoped to prove that locking up Japanese Americans violated their rights.

The ACLU supported Mexican Americans students, like those pictured here, who were forced to attend segregated schools in the 1940s. Mexican American activists protested this segregation, and won a court case that ended it in California and Southwestern states.

When Ernest explained to Fred that the case could take a while, he meant that there could be many stages in the court process. If a judge ruled that Fred was guilty of disobeying the government, Fred could appeal the judge's decision. If necessary, Fred could appeal all the way to the United States Supreme Court. The judges on that court would make the final decision.

HAVE YOU EVER BEEN AN ALLY TO SOMEONE WHO NEEDED HELP?

APPEAL:
to request a more powerful court to review a decision made by a less powerful court.

An Ally in Camp

Ralph Lazo was of Mexican and Irish ancestry, and he had many Nisei friends at his Los Angeles high school. He thought it was wrong for the government to force Japanese Americans into prison camps. To support his friends and to protest their unfair treatment, he chose to live with them at the prison camp called Manzanar. In this picture, Ralph is on the right, shaking hands with one of his Nisei friends in a classroom at Manzanar.

Ralph was an ally to Japanese Americans by remaining loyal to his friends and showing them that not everyone turned their backs on Japanese Americans. Other allies took care of Japanese American families' farms and businesses while they were imprisoned. It was brave to be an ally to Japanese Americans during this time.

TIMELINE

1920
ACLU is founded.

1942
Early June
Fred meets Ernest Besig.

June 18
Fred appears in court in San Francisco.

1947
Mexican American activists win their court case ending segregation of Mexican Americans in California and the Southwest.

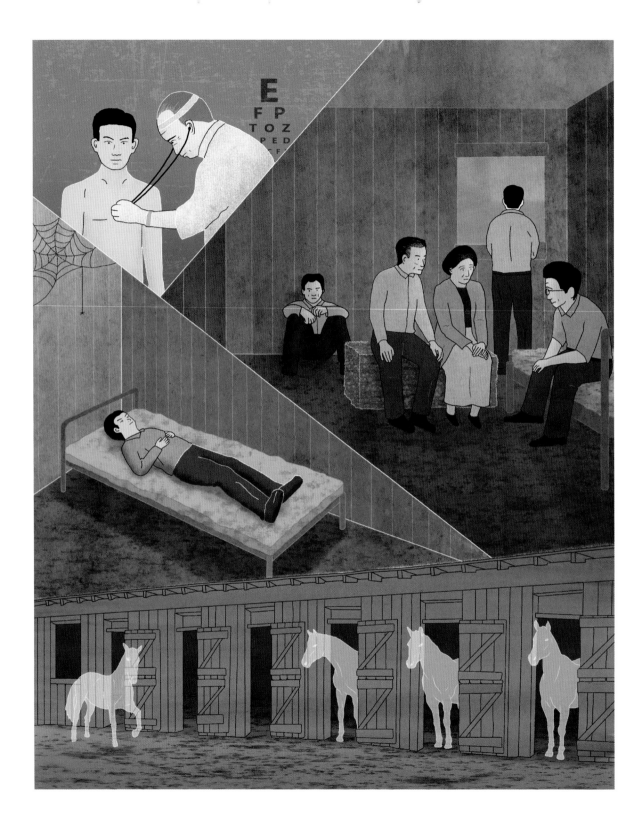

7.
LIVING IN A HORSE STALL

Tanforan.
Just weeks ago
a racetrack where
horses galloped.
Now a prison camp
for humans.

Barbed wire surrounds the entrance.
Men with guns stand guard.
The smell of horse manure
punches Fred in the face.

Government workers fingerprint him
and examine him for diseases.

He left jail only to become
a prisoner again.

Fred is taken to a room
stinking of horses:
dirt floor,
holes in the walls,
gap under the door,
one bare lightbulb,
an iron cot for a bed.

A horse stall.

Fred lies down.
This was made for horses,
not for human beings, he thinks.
Jail was a lot better than this.

Nearly eight thousand
Japanese Americans lived
in the horse stalls and other
buildings at Tanforan.

Then his brother Hi
knocks on the door.
Ma and Pa want to see you.
You better come along.

Fred finds his family
on the other side of the racetrack
in a room just as cramped.
They have covered the cracks with newspapers
and hung blankets to create walls.
As homey as they can make it.

Fred's family knows
that he was arrested
and that he plans to fight the government
for imprisoning Japanese Americans.

But they do not feel proud of him.

His father is disgusted.
Dumbell, he says.
Why did you do such a thing?

Fred sees the shame
hovering around his mother.
She doesn't want to leave their room,
afraid of what others will say
about what Fred is doing.

But his parents still insist
that he move in with them.

Once again
Fred feels like an outsider
even as they all cram together
in the tiny room.

There is a meeting
of young men at Tanforan
to discuss if they think Fred should continue
to fight against his imprisonment.

Several gather,
talking among themselves.
When Fred walks up,
they turn their backs.

He gets the message:
Do what you want
but we will not support you.

They are afraid
his fight will make things even harder
for Japanese Americans.

But Fred knows he is speaking up
for what is right.

Then Ida writes to Fred
saying she can't visit him,
and later that she can't even
write to him anymore.
She worries that it will
get her into trouble.

So Fred stops reaching out to Ida.
He doesn't want to hurt her.
He lets go of his dreams
of their future together.
And he never sees her again.

Fred is surrounded by so many people.

Yet he is
all
alone.

LIFE IN A PRISON CAMP

The government sent Fred's family and all the other Japanese Americans in and around San Francisco to live on the grounds of a horse-racing track called Tanforan, just south of San Francisco. There were thirteen of these sites up and down the West Coast. Armed soldiers guarded the camp to prevent Japanese Americans from leaving. At night, they scanned the camp with bright searchlights to make sure no one tried to escape.

Japanese Americans arriving at Tanforan had to wait for government officials to search their belongings, take their fingerprints, examine them for diseases, and assign them rooms. This photograph shows the stands of the racetrack, where visitors once cheered for their favorite horses.

After finding out where in Tanforan they would live, Japanese Americans often had to stuff straw into large cloth bags to make their mattresses.

Japanese Americans lived in small, cramped rooms at Tanforan. This elderly man shared two small rooms with his two sons, his daughter, and his daughter's husband.

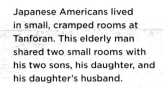

People had to wait in long lines to eat in large mess halls.

Nisei artist Miné Okubo drew pictures of her experiences at Tanforan. In this drawing she shows how people had to use shared bathrooms. There was very little privacy.

When Fred arrived at Tanforan, many Japanese Americans didn't support him. He had been in jail, so some considered Fred to be a criminal. Others believed that Japanese Americans should prove their loyalty to the United States by obeying the government's orders. Some thought Fred's fight against the government made him seem disloyal. He could make all Japanese Americans look disloyal too.

At Tanforan, Fred also got bad news about his case. A judge had decided he was guilty of disobeying the orders to go to the prison camp. Now, he had been officially convicted of a crime. But Fred and Ernest appealed that judge's decision. This meant that a more powerful court would review Fred's case.

HAVE YOU EVER DISAGREED WITH YOUR FAMILY OR FRIENDS ABOUT SOMETHING IMPORTANT TO YOU?

TIMELINE — 1942

April 28
Tanforan is converted from a racetrack into a temporary prison camp.

June
Fred is imprisoned at Tanforan.

September 8
A judge rules that Fred disobeyed the law. Fred's lawyer appeals.

8.
FEELING
LIKE
AN ORPHAN

September 1942.
Fred and his family
are pushed onto a train,
rattling on tracks for two days.
They climb out into searing heat
at another prison camp.

Topaz sprawls in the Utah desert
on land that no one else wants,
designed like a small city.

How long does the government
expect them to be here?

Fred, his brothers, and his parents
squeeze into two small rooms.
Their new address:
Block 28
Building 9
Rooms C and D.

Fred and Ernest write letters
back and forth.
A friendship grows.

Just a little wind and the dust rises like fog
all over the Relocation Center,
Fred writes to Ernest.
You can't see ten feet in front of you.
We all have to wear masks made of cloth.

He digs ditches
to help build a hospital,
but the men he works with
are not friendly.

They believe that Fred thinks
he is different
from the rest of them—
that he's more White
than Japanese.

Fred eats his meals alone,
waiting for news about his case.

If the courts
decide in his favor,
then all that he has lost—
his car
his girlfriend
his freedom—
will have been worth it.

Fred wrote this letter to
Ernest describing the
terrible dust at Topaz.

November 1942.
The government
lets some Japanese Americans
work outside of the camp
on seasonal permits.

Fred gets a job picking sugar beets,
bent over for hours,
dirt stuck under his fingernails
and on his skin.

But at least he is working
outside of barbed wire.

Then, Fred applies to leave Topaz for good
and is allowed to move to Salt Lake City.
Factories turn him away
because he looks like the enemy.
He finally finds work as a welder.

Just over a year ago,
Fred was driving his Pontiac
and reading the comics with Ida—
gazing at the San Francisco Bay
spread out like an invitation.

I don't even know how it is
to have a home,
Fred writes to Ernest.
I feel like an orphan.

TRYING TO BE FREE AGAIN

The government used Tanforan as a temporary site for Japanese Americans in the San Francisco Bay Area while it built longer-term camps in remote parts of the country. When they were completed, the government forced Japanese Americans to move to these bigger prison camps that were surrounded by barbed wire and guarded by soldiers with guns.

The government ultimately imprisoned 120,000 Japanese Americans—some for as long as three years. Most of them were born in the United States and were American citizens. Many were children and elderly people. Babies were born in these camps. Old and sick people died in them, far from their homes.

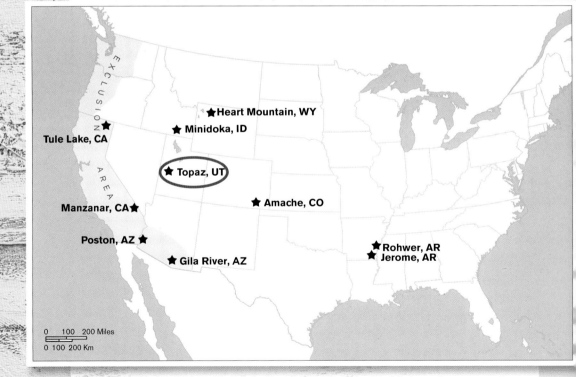

Topaz, where the government imprisoned more than eight thousand people, was one of ten larger camps throughout the United States.

The Topaz prison camp covered one square mile and was divided into forty-two blocks. Most of the blocks had twelve barracks, each of which was separated into small rooms where people lived, a dining hall, a recreation hall, and a shared bathroom and laundry facility.

BARRACKS: large plain buildings for soldiers or others to live in, often for a short period of time.

As the war continued, the government eventually let many Japanese Americans out of Topaz and the other camps for short periods to work nearby. Later, people who declared their loyalty to the United States and had a job or college waiting for them could leave for longer periods. But they still could not go to the West Coast. And even though they were no longer living in the prison camps, they had to report their movements to the government.

Fred left Topaz as soon as he could. He moved to Salt Lake City, 130 miles north of Topaz, in December 1942.

The Power of Words

What does the word "evacuation" mean to you?

The United States government used the word "evacuation" to describe forcing Japanese Americans from their homes and into prison camps. "Evacuation" means leaving a dangerous place for your own safety—like during an earthquake, fire, or hurricane. In using the word "evacuation," the government made its actions against Japanese Americans seem harmless. The government called places like Tanforan "assembly centers." What does it mean to assemble? Think of a school assembly. You go willingly—because you want to be there.

No one wanted to live in these camps.

The government called the more permanent camps like Topaz "relocation centers," not "prisons," even though they were surrounded by barbed wire and armed guards. If the government had called the camps "prisons," do you think it would have affected how other Americans thought about what was happening to Japanese Americans?

Like Fred, Miné Okubo was imprisoned at Topaz. In this drawing she shows fierce winds whipping up a dust storm. During the summer, temperatures at Topaz could rise well above 100 degrees. In the winter, ice covered the ground.

This drawing by artist Chiura Obata shows an Issei man named Hatsuki Wakasa who was shot and killed at Topaz by a prison guard because he was walking near the fence. Japanese Americans at Topaz were shocked, sad, and angry about the shooting. They knew they could be killed for doing something as harmless as walking near the barbed-wire fence.

april 11th 1943
Hatsuki Wakasa
Shot by M.P.

Enduring Hardship

Many Japanese Americans trapped in camps like Topaz created art about their experiences. A young girl named Kimii Nagata wrote this poem.

Be Like the Cactus

Let not harsh tongues, that wag in vain,

Discourage you. In spite of pain,

Be like the cactus, which through rain,

And storm, and thunder, can remain.

TIMELINE

1942

September 28
Fred is transferred from Tanforan to Topaz.

November
Fred gets leave from Topaz to pick sugar beets.

December
Fred leaves Topaz for Salt Lake City.

1943

April 11
Hatsuki Wakasa is shot and killed at Topaz.

9.
GETTING
THE LETTER

All the time Fred wonders
about his case,
which moves from one court to the next.

February 1943.
Fred writes to Ernest,
*I am very anxious to hear
the outcome of our case.*

Ernest replies that
it could take a long time
for the case to reach
the United States Supreme Court.

Fred waits.

March 1944.
The Supreme Court
agrees to hear Fred's case.
The lawyers will present their arguments
in October.

Nice going,
Fred writes to Ernest.

Fred waits.

October 1944.
Fred moves to Detroit,
where he finds work making doors
for navy ships
and lives in a room at the YMCA.

December 1944.
Fred finally receives the letter from Ernest—
the one he has been waiting for.

He tears it open
and reads Ernest's words.

They
lost.

Six of nine judges ruled
that it was legal to
remove Japanese Americans
from their homes
because of "military necessity."

Fred can't believe it.
How could the court decide that
the government was right
to tear these people
away from their lives
for looking like the enemy—
not for doing anything wrong?

Two long years
fighting this fight
for the country he loves—
his own country—
and Fred has lost.

Am I an American or not?
he wonders.

He has lost Ida,
his friends,
his home.

Fred now feels
as if he has lost
his country.

Fred's letter to Ernest after hearing about the Supreme Court's decision. Wayne Collins, mentioned in the letter, was a lawyer who helped to fight Fred's case.

BEHIND THE COURT'S DECISION

When the United States Supreme Court agreed to hear Fred's appeal, Fred's lawyers were determined to convince the nine judges that imprisoning Japanese Americans violated their constitutional rights. At the same time, government lawyers set out to show the judges that there were good reasons to force Japanese Americans from their homes.

In making their decision, the judges on the Supreme Court looked at a report by Lieutenant General John L. DeWitt, the military commander in charge of the West Coast. The report said there was a risk that Japanese Americans were sending signals to Japanese Empire ships and submarines in the Pacific Ocean. DeWitt said that there wasn't enough time to figure out if individual Japanese Americans were loyal to the United States. Most of the judges on the Supreme Court agreed with the government that it was a "military necessity" to force Japanese Americans to leave their homes.

Not all of the Supreme Court judges thought the government was right to imprison Fred and other Japanese Americans. Three of the nine judges agreed with Fred. They believed that the government's actions were racist and violated Japanese Americans' rights. But because the Supreme Court rules by majority, which means that more than half of the judges need to agree on a decision, Fred lost his case.

The nine judges on the United States Supreme Court who decided Fred's case.

Newspapers across the country carried the news that the United States Supreme Court had ruled against Fred and decided that the government could force thousands of people from their homes if they looked like the enemy.

KOREMATSU v. UNITED STATES.

CERTIORARI TO THE CIRCUIT COURT OF APPEALS FOR THE NINTH CIRCUIT.

No. 22. Argued October 11, 12, 1944.—Decided December 18, 1944.

1. Civilian Exclusion Order No. 34 which, during a state of war with Japan and as a protection against espionage and sabotage, was promulgated by the Commanding General of the Western Defense Command under authority of Executive Order No. 9066 and the Act of March 21, 1942, and which directed the exclusion after May 9, 1942 from a described West Coast military area of all persons of Japanese ancestry, *held* constitutional as of the time it was made and when the petitioner—an American citizen of Japanese descent whose home was in the described area—violated it. P. 219.

2. The provisions of other orders requiring persons of Japanese ancestry to report to assembly centers and providing for the detention of such persons in assembly and relocation centers were separate, and their validity is not in issue in this proceeding. P. 222.

When the Supreme Court makes a ruling, the judges write out the reasons why they reached their decision. This is from the Supreme Court's official ruling in Fred's case.

Fred was devastated by the decision. The court had ruled that the government could force a group of people from their homes because of their race and ancestry, as long as there was "military necessity." The government could use the same excuse to violate people's rights in the future.

TIMELINE – 1944

March 27
Supreme Court agrees to hear Fred's case.

October
Fred moves to Detroit.

December 18
Supreme Court rules against Fred.

10.
REBUILDING, 1945 TO 1966

The war ends.
The camps close.
Japanese Americans
try to rebuild their lives.

Fred meets Kathryn,
a smart woman from South Carolina,
full of curiosity
with two college degrees in science.
They date through the summer,
snuggling to music from the radio,
and dancing at Detroit's Eastwood Gardens.

Kathryn knows about Fred's case
and agrees that he was right
to fight for justice.

Fred has found a new love
and a partner for life.

They get married—
legally in Michigan.

It would still be illegal in California
since Fred is Japanese American and
Kathryn is White.

Then they move to Oakland,
Fred's hometown,
and have two children,
Karen and Ken.

Fred adores being a dad.
Karen and Ken both become Scouts
just like Fred and Walt used to be.
Fred is always there to cheer for Ken
at his Little League baseball games
and for Karen at her ballet recitals.
They love to watch the San Francisco Giants—
their favorite baseball team—
on their big-box TV.

The whole family goes to church
and Fred becomes a proud member
of the Lions Club,
raising money for people who need help.

Fred works as a draftsman,
drawing plans for buildings.
Because he lost his case
and was convicted of a crime,
there are some jobs he cannot get,
like working for a big company.
So Fred takes two jobs
to be able to buy a home and
care for his family.

A family.
The life Fred dreamed about.

When Karen is sixteen and a junior
at San Lorenzo High School,
her friend Maya gives a report
on Japanese American prison camps.

Maya mentions a Supreme Court case
Korematsu v. United States.
After Karen's last name rings out,
thirty-five pairs of eyes stare at her.

This is the first time Karen has even heard
about the camps.

Who is this Korematsu?
Karen wonders.
Maybe a distant relative?

She rushes home
and asks her mother,
What's this about?

Her mother tells Karen
that it was her father's case.

Her father?
Her quiet, law-abiding,
church-going father?
Karen can't believe it.

Why didn't anybody tell me?
Karen asks.

Her mother says that Fred was concerned
that she was too young
to understand.
Karen can talk to him
when he gets home.

Hours later and the sun goes down.
Karen waits.

Finally, Fred walks through the door
and Karen asks him about the case.

He tells her that it happened long ago.
The United States Supreme Court ruled against him,
but he believes he did the right thing.

Karen can see that he has
a hard time telling her
even this little bit.

AFTER IMPRISONMENT

World War II ended when the Empire of Japan surrendered in August 1945. The government finally allowed Japanese Americans to return to the West Coast. But most of them had no homes or jobs. They faced anger and sometimes attacks from people who did not want them back.

Fred's parents and brothers returned to their nursery, where they found hundreds of shattered glass windowpanes in the greenhouses. The buildings were falling apart because the tenants who had rented their nursery had not taken care of it.

HAVE YOU EVER LEARNED SOMETHING ABOUT YOUR FAMILY THAT SURPRISED YOU?

Daniel Inouye won medals for his bravery during World War II. He lost his right arm due to battle injuries. After the war, he wanted to get a haircut in Oakland. The barber told him, "We don't cut Jap hair." Inouye thought to himself, "Here I am in uniform. It should be obvious to him that I'm an American soldier.... And he's telling me we don't cut Jap hair." Years later, Inouye became a United States Senator for the state of Hawai'i.

Like thousands of other Japanese Americans, Fred worked hard to resume his life after the war. But Fred had an additional challenge. He had been found guilty of breaking the law by refusing to report to the prison camp at Tanforan. The government and many businesses would not hire someone who had been convicted of breaking the law.

Sometimes when Fred and Kathryn were alone, he told her of his secret wish that he could reopen his case and get his conviction overturned. But he didn't know how that could ever happen.

Fred, Kathryn, Karen, and Ken Korematsu in 1966, the year that Karen found out about Fred's case. Japanese Americans who had been imprisoned during World War II rarely talked about that experience, even to their children. It was too upsetting for many of them.

TIMELINE

1945

August 14
Japan surrenders and World War II ends.

December 17
Japanese Americans are allowed to return to the West Coast.

1946
Fred and Kathryn marry in Detroit.

Movements for Justice

Reverend Martin Luther King Jr. (front row, second from left) and other activists marching in Washington, DC, for equal rights.

While Japanese Americans were rebuilding their lives, other groups in the United States were protesting discrimination and unfair treatment.

During the 1950s and 1960s, African American activists and their allies created a nation-wide movement to fight against racial segregation and unfair laws. Because of their hard work and determination, the government finally passed the Civil Rights Act in 1964. This law made discrimination based on race, color, ancestry, or religion illegal in hotels, restaurants, and other businesses—including barbershops.

MOVEMENT: a group of people working together to change something important to them.

Around the same time, Mexican American and Filipino American activists built a movement to fight for the rights of farmworkers. These Latino and Filipino laborers picked most of the fruits and vegetables for the United States, but were treated unfairly because of their race and ancestry. Farmworkers and their allies protested. Eventually, some farmworkers got fairer pay and safer working conditions.

Farmworkers and their allies protesting unfair working conditions and low pay.

1964
Civil Rights Act is passed.

1966
Karen learns about her father's case.

1970
Farmworkers begin to get fairer pay and safer working conditions.

11.
UNCOVERING LIES, 1982

One January morning
Fred receives a phone call.
A man named Peter Irons
wants to meet with him.
He has new information
about Fred's case.

It has been nearly forty years since
the United States Supreme Court
ruled against Fred.

Though several people have
asked him to talk
about what happened,
Fred has almost always said no.

Now
Fred says
yes.

Peter arrives with a tape recorder in hand
and gives Fred documents to read.
Peter found them in the
National Archives—
the place where government papers
are kept.

Fred reads page after page
silently
for thirty minutes.

He finds out that people in the military
and lawyers for the government
lied.

They had no evidence
that Japanese Americans
were spies or a risk to the country.

The whole case was built on lies.
Lies that locked up Fred,
his family, and
120,000 Japanese Americans.

Lies that stole toys from children
and pets from families.

Lies that ripped people from their lives
and then threw them back in
without homes or jobs.

Fred puts down the papers.

They did me a great wrong,
he says.

Peter tells him that it is possible
to reopen Fred's case
based on these documents.

Are you a lawyer?
Fred asks.

Yes, I am.

Would you like to be my lawyer?
Fred asks.

A team of lawyers gather
and get to work.
Most of them are young Japanese Americans,
children of people who were imprisoned.

When they first crowd into
Fred and Kathryn's living room
Fred leans over and whispers to Peter,
Hey, these look like high school kids.

Oh no, they're the best,
Peter replies.

When Fred sees them in action
he agrees
and the team becomes
part of the Korematsu family.

The lawyers
work for no money,
but from a firm belief
that it is time for the truth to be told.

Almost two years pass
as they gather evidence
and figure out the best way
to challenge Fred's conviction.

At first Fred stays in the background
letting the lawyers do the talking.
Then he decides it is important
to step forward.

When he speaks
out loud again
about what happened to him
and other Japanese Americans,
his courage glows through
his no-nonsense words
and quiet voice.

REOPENING THE CASE

Professor Peter Irons and researcher Aiko Herzig-Yoshinaga found papers in dusty boxes at the National Archives proving that the United States government's lawyers had lied to the Supreme Court. The lawyers had told the judges that there were reasons to believe that Japanese Americans were signaling to enemy ships and submarines. In fact, these lawyers had read reports that there was *no* evidence of Japanese Americans signaling to the enemy, and that almost all Japanese Americans were loyal to the United States.

But the government's lawyers did not give these reports to the Supreme Court. Instead, they lied and said that the opposite was true. This was government misconduct.

Had the judges on the Supreme Court known the truth, Fred might have won his case.

Aiko Herzig-Yoshinaga.   Peter Irons.

NATIONAL ARCHIVES:
the part of the United States government that houses government records and documents.

GOVERNMENT MISCONDUCT:
behavior by the government that is legally or morally wrong.

This memo from one government lawyer to another is one of the documents that Peter Irons and Aiko Herzig-Yoshinaga found. In this memo written in 1944, lawyer Edward Ennis explains that Lieutenant General John L. DeWitt's report contained lies, and that there was no evidence that Japanese Americans were sending messages to the enemy. The report was still presented to the Supreme Court, even though the government knew it was untrue.

> The wilful historical inaccuracies of the report are objectionable for two different reasons. (1) The chief argument in the report as to the necessity for the evacuation is that the Department of Justice was slow in enforcing alien enemy control measures and that it would not take the necessary steps to prevent signaling whether by radio or by lights. It asserts that radio transmitters were located within general areas but this Department would not permit mass searches to find them. It asserts that signaling was observed in mixed occupancy dwellings which this Department would not permit to be entered. Thus, because this Department would not allow the reasonable and less drastic measures which General DeWitt wished, he was forced to evacuate the entire population. The argument is untrue both with respect to what this Department did and with respect to the radio transmissions and signaling, none of which existed, as General DeWitt at the time well knew. (2) The report asserts that the Japanese-Americans were engaged in extensive radio signaling and in shore-to-ship signaling. The general tenor of the report is not only to the effect that there was a reason to be apprehensive, but also to the effect that overt acts of treason were being committed. Since this is not so it is highly unfair to this racial minority that these lies, put out in an official publication, go uncorrected. This is the only opportunity which this Department has to correct them.

Because of what Peter and Aiko had discovered, Fred had the rare opportunity to reopen his case. Ernest Besig had been Fred's ally all those years earlier, helping him to fight for justice. Now, Peter, Aiko, and the other lawyers who helped Fred reopen his case became his allies too.

When Fred decided to reopen the case, he took a risk. If a judge ruled against Fred, he would face the disappointment of losing all over again. The loss might also hurt Japanese Americans as a group. Nisei and Sansei activists were trying to pass a law to make the United States government apologize to Japanese Americans who had been wrongfully imprisoned during World War II, and to pay them reparations for their losses and suffering. If Fred lost his case again, it might hurt their effort.

In the 1970s and 1980s, many Japanese Americans began speaking up about the hardships they had suffered in prison camps, and how the experience had torn their lives apart. In this picture, Japanese American activists and their allies are marching for justice and reparations.

But if Fred won, he would not only clear his own name. He would also help prevent the government from treating other groups unfairly in the future.

Many of the Japanese American lawyers who helped Fred reopen his case had parents who had been in prison camps. Some of Fred's lawyers are in this picture. Bottom row, from left: Dale Minami, Fred Korematsu, Peter Irons. Back row, from left: Don Tamaki, Dennis Hayashi, Lorraine Bannai.

IF YOU FAILED AT SOMETHING, HAVE YOU EVER TAKEN A BIG RISK TO TRY AGAIN?

TIMELINE

1981
September
Peter Irons and Aiko Herzig-Yoshinaga find documents showing the government lied.

1982
January 12
Fred meets Peter Irons.

1983
January 31
Fred and his lawyers officially reopen his case.

Fred Korematsu

12.
MAKING THE CASE, 1983

Fred and Kathryn push through
a blustery wind to enter
the tall Federal Court Building
near San Francisco's City Hall.

In the courtroom
every seat is filled with people
who have waited since eight in the morning
to come in.

Japanese Americans—
some who lived in the prison camps—
are crowded onto benches
anywhere there is a seat.

When Fred first went to court
many of these people
thought he was wrong
to challenge the government.

They turned their backs on Fred.

Now they think differently.
Fred isn't alone anymore.

But what will the judge decide?

The lawyers speak
and then Fred rises
to stand before the judge.

If he loses
he will let
so many people down.

His voice is soft but firm.

Your Honor, I still remember
forty years ago when I was handcuffed
and arrested as a criminal.

We can never forget this incident
as long as we live.
The horse stalls that we stayed in were
made for horses,
not human beings.

As long as my record stands in federal court,
any American citizen can be held in prison
or concentration camp without a trial or hearing.
That is, if they look like the enemy of this country.

Therefore, I would like to see the government admit
that they were wrong and do something about it

so this will never happen again to any American citizen
of any race, creed, or color.

Judge Patel shuffles her papers.
It feels like there is electricity in the air.
The walls almost vibrate
with the silence in the room.

Then she speaks
in complicated legal language
that Fred doesn't understand.

He turns to one of his lawyers and asks
what happened.

Fred, you won.
You won your case!

Fred is quiet.

Then he says,
That's good.
That's really good.

People crowd around Fred
crying and laughing,
shaking his hand and
giving him hugs.

In 1942, when Fred sat alone in a jail cell,
he never dreamed that
forty years later he would be
congratulated as a hero.

Fred challenged something
he thought was unfair.

He spoke up—
for himself
and for all Japanese Americans,
even when no one stood with him.

It was not easy.
But Fred fought
to make the United States—
his country—
a fairer place.

And he won.

We all won.

FRED'S FIGHT FOR JUSTICE

Judge Marilyn Hall Patel agreed with Fred's lawyers: the government's lawyers had lied to the United States Supreme Court. They did not have evidence that there was a "military necessity" to imprison Japanese Americans. She overturned Fred's conviction for not reporting to prison camp.

It was an important victory, not just for Fred, but also for Japanese Americans and all Americans. Finally, a judge had ruled that it was wrong for the government to force Japanese Americans out of their homes and lock them up. Now it would be harder in the future for the government to put people behind barbed wire just because they looked like the enemy.

Judge Marilyn Hall Patel.

Many Japanese Americans had changed their minds about Fred in the forty years since World War II. Over time, they realized that questioning the government's actions did not make them disloyal to their country. They recognized how brave and determined Fred had been.

Fred and his friend and ally Ernest Besig, 1989.

HOW CAN ONE PERSON, WITH HELP FROM ALLIES, MAKE A DIFFERENCE?

Fred had finally won his case in court. But his work was not done. Fred hoped that government officials would never again unfairly target any group, like they had targeted Japanese Americans during World War II. But he knew it could happen again.

So, Fred traveled across the United States to talk to people about what the government had done to Japanese Americans and about his experience fighting that injustice. He spoke to hundreds of people, young and old, including students, teachers, and government leaders.

On January 15, 1998, President Bill Clinton honored Fred Korematsu with the Presidential Medal of Freedom, the highest civilian award for an American.

Later, Fred told Karen he wished his parents could have been there.

Fred shaking hands with President Bill Clinton, who told him, "It was a very brave thing that you did to stand up against the government."

APOLOGY

THE WHITE HOUSE
WASHINGTON

A monetary sum and words alone cannot restore lost years or erase painful memories; neither can they fully convey our Nation's resolve to rectify injustice and to uphold the rights of individuals. We can never fully right the wrongs of the past. But we can take a clear stand for justice and recognize that serious injustices were done to Japanese Americans during World War II.

In enacting a law calling for restitution and offering a sincere apology, your fellow Americans have, in a very real sense, renewed their traditional commitment to the ideals of freedom, equality, and justice. You and your family have our best wishes for the future.

Sincerely,

GEORGE BUSH
PRESIDENT OF THE UNITED STATES

OCTOBER 1990

Five years after Fred won his case, Japanese American activists convinced the government to pass the Civil Liberties Act of 1988. The United States government publicly apologized, admitting that imprisoning innocent Japanese Americans was wrong. This law also provided a reparations payment of $20,000 to each Japanese American still living who had been imprisoned during World War II. Fred and Kathryn worked with hundreds of other activists to get this law passed.

TERRORIST:
a person who uses terror or violence to scare people into change.

After receiving the Presidential Medal of Freedom, Fred continued to speak up. His message was: Do not let what happened to Japanese Americans happen to anyone else. He told his listeners, "You always have to watch out about protecting your rights."

After September 11, 2001, Fred's message became even more important. Early that morning, terrorists from Middle Eastern countries crashed planes into the World Trade Center towers in New York City. Thousands of people died.

The World Trade Center burning after the terrorist attacks on September 11, 2001.

Americans were shocked and afraid, just like they had been after the attack on Pearl Harbor in 1941. Back then, people turned against Japanese Americans because they looked like the enemy. In 2001, many Americans turned against immigrants and Americans of Middle Eastern ancestry because they looked like the terrorists.

Fred spoke up against this unfairness. "No one should ever be locked away simply because they share the same race, ethnicity, or religion as a spy or terrorist," he said. Fred learned that the United States government had imprisoned hundreds of Middle Eastern men without giving them trials. After these men asked the United States Supreme Court to give them a chance to prove their innocence, Fred supported them.

Fred spent the rest of his life speaking up for the rights of others and fighting for justice for all people. He died on March 30, 2005.

✿ ✿ ✿

TIMELINE

1983
November 10
Judge Patel overturns
Fred's conviction.

1988
August 10
Civil Liberties Act is passed.

1998
January 15
President Clinton awards Fred
the Presidential Medal
of Freedom.

Fred Korematsu, 1919–2005.

2001
September 11
World Trade Center is attacked.

2005
March 30
Fred dies.

SPEAKING UP FOR JUSTICE: FROM FRED'S DAY TO OURS

HOW CAN YOU BE LIKE FRED AND SPEAK UP FOR WHAT YOU THINK IS RIGHT?

When you look around your school or your community, do you see people being treated badly? When you watch the news or read the newspapers, do you learn about situations that don't seem fair or right?

Fred made the choice to speak up against unfairness. He took a lot of risks in speaking up. He also found allies who helped him along the way.

In the end, Fred helped to make the United States a fairer place for everyone.

We all make choices, and these choices can be important. We can speak up when we see something that isn't fair, or when someone else is being treated badly.

Anyone, big or small, loud or quiet, young or old, can speak up. We can speak up through our actions or our words, to one person or to many.

And we can all make a difference—in our family, in our school, in our community, and in our world.

Ideas for Young Activists

Kids are often the first to see when something isn't fair or right, and can come up with exciting ideas and creative actions. Once you've found an issue that is important to you, here are some ideas for next steps that you can take.

GET INFORMATION

Is there a person or group of people who are being treated badly? Is there a rule that seems unfair? Is there someone in a position to change things for the better?

Read more about the topic. Research the situation so you feel that you really understand it. Be clear about the kind of change you'd like to see.

TALK ABOUT IT

Talk to the people around you about what you've learned. This could include your friends, your family, your teachers, and your classmates. Start a discussion and gather ideas about what you and your friends can do.

TAKE ACTION

There are lots of different ways to speak up. Here are just a few ideas:

❀ Create a group to meet regularly and come up with plans to address your issue. It can be fun to work together.

❀ Organize a letter-writing campaign to someone who has the power to make a difference in your community. This could be the head of a company or an elected official who helps to make laws.

❀ Raise money to fund an organization that is fighting for the change you want to see. Sell cookies, make crafts, run a lemonade stand—these are just a few examples. And be sure to spread the word about why you are raising money.

❀ Come up with your own creative solution. Think about what you like to do, and figure out a way to combine that with speaking up and fighting for change. If you like to sing or dance, put on a play with your friends to raise awareness. If you are artistic, create something that speaks to the issue you care about, then display it at your school or post it online. If you play a sport, organize a sporting event with your issue as the theme. The sky is the limit!

❀ Organize a Fred Korematsu Day event at your school (turn the page to learn more).

SHARE YOUR PROGRESS

Let people know about your challenges and successes. You can create a blog or website, or write to your local newspapers. People will want to know what you have achieved. You can inspire them to know that they can make a difference too.

Resources

Here are some websites where you can learn more about your rights and ways to take action around issues that matter to you.

iCivics: Founded by former Supreme Court Justice Sandra Day O'Connor, iCivics has tons of online resources for kids who want to learn about government, law, and our rights as citizens. Play fun, animated games and see how you stack up among students across the country. www.icivics.org.

ACLU: In the "Know Your Rights" section, you can learn about the rights all Americans have, and also about groups who are facing discrimination. This can help you to know when your rights, or the rights of others, are being violated. www.aclu.org/know-your-rights.

Do Something: This is one of the largest global organizations supporting young people and social change. The site allows you to select the kind of issue you want to address, how much time you have, and the type of activism you want to engage in. www.dosomething.org.

Inspire My Kids: Looking for more ideas? This site features kids who are making a difference in all kinds of places, in all kinds of ways. You can explore by values, topics, subjects, and age range. There's plenty of food for thought on ways to change the world. inspiremykids.com.

MY FATHER

by Karen Korematsu

My father lived by his principles of right and wrong. He learned about the Constitution in high school and assumed he had civil rights as an American citizen. Fred Korematsu's story is not just a West Coast story or a story about the Japanese American incarceration. It is an American story.

George Santayana said, "Those who do not learn from history are doomed to repeat it." Fred Korematsu's story is the reminder of the constant danger that the government will overreach unless the public and the courts are vigilant.

My father gave me the charge to carry on his legacy through education, as he felt that education is so important to our future in this world.

January 30 is my father's birthday and also "Fred Korematsu Day of Civil Liberties and the Constitution." This is the first statewide day in US history named after an Asian American, first established in California beginning on January 30, 2011. Now other states have followed, and there is a grassroots movement to establish "Fred Korematsu Day of Civil Liberties and the Constitution" as a national federal holiday.

I founded the Fred T. Korematsu Institute before the first Fred Korematsu Day was formed. Now we have created "Korematsu Institute Teaching Kits" that teachers may order free of charge through our website, www.korematsuinstitute.org, and we encourage students to use our website as a resource. We have sent our teaching kits to all fifty states and to seven countries. Other countries view Fred Korematsu's story and the Japanese American Incarceration as a human rights violation.

Fred Korematsu is one person who made a difference, and, dear reader, SO CAN YOU! My father was not born an American civil rights hero. He became one, just like Martin Luther King Jr., Cesar Chavez, and Rosa Parks. I would encourage you to learn about your own history, where your family came from, and the struggles they may have had in the past and even now. Hopefully, when you know your own history, you can appreciate the struggles of others. If we are to move forward and find peace in this country and around the world, we must learn to RESPECT each other and our differences.

My father said, "Protest, but not with violence; otherwise they won't listen to you. But don't be afraid to speak up!" If you see someone being bullied, either in person or on social media, or if you see or experience discrimination, remember Fred Korematsu. He is my inspiration, and I hope he will be yours too.

FRED KOREMATSU DAY
OF CIVIL LIBERTIES AND THE CONSTITUTION

STANDUPFORWHATISRIGHT

JANUARY 30 OF EVERY YEAR
www.korematsuinstitute.org

ACKNOWLEDGMENTS

We are deeply grateful to the many people who assisted us with this book. We thank Karen Korematsu and Ken Korematsu for telling us about their father and for enabling us to relate his story. Lorraine K. Bannai, author of *Enduring Conviction: Fred Korematsu and His Quest for Justice*, very generously shared research materials and insights from her definitive biography of Fred Korematsu. Educator Barb Wenger helped on many levels, from organizing a focus group of teachers to guiding us on how to present Fred's story to a young audience.

Several educators, librarians, and writers helped us to shape the content of this book and to frame the series of which it is a part: Jennifer Brouhard, Jessica Login, Dana Wahlberg, Kristi Moos, Viet Nguyen, Greg John, Elizabeth Partridge, Nicole Geiger, Carrie Donovan, Rachel Reinhard, Sandy Brumbaum, and Carla Reimer. Others provided helpful feedback on drafts: Karen Boyden, Libbie Schock, Christine Leishman, Lorraine Bannai, Brian Niiya, Jane Kurtz, and Katie Van Ark. We appreciate their valuable comments and suggestions.

Librarian Heidi Bartsch and teacher Debra Cruger-Hansen organized a focus group of fourth-grade students at Mira Vista School in Richmond, California. We thank them and the following students for helping us to tell Fred's story: Gurtej, Lily, Matias, Meridith, Rosie, Sanai, Sebastian, and Zhia.

Alison Moore provided expert assistance at the California Historical Society, the repository for the archives of the ACLU of Northern California, which includes correspondence between Fred Korematsu and Ernest Besig. J.K. Yamamoto of the *Rafu Shimpo* and Patricia Biggs of the Manzanar National Historic Site were very helpful with photo research. Mary Yogi of the Los Angeles County Public Library accessed newspaper archives for us. Milton Reynolds and Mary Hendra of Facing History and Ourselves suggested resources for activism and civics education. Eric Paul Fournier generously shared the transcript for his award-winning film *Of Civil Wrongs and Rights: The Fred Korematsu Story.*

The stellar team at Heyday was critical to the creation of this book. Publisher Malcolm Margolin came up with the idea for a series of children's books about civil liberties heroes and heroines. Editorial Director Gayle Wattawa provided useful suggestions and asked rigorous questions throughout the process of developing the book. Illustrator Yutaka Houlette helped to bring Fred Korematsu to life on the page, while designer Nancy Austin and art director Diane Lee brought the book together visually. Editor Molly Woodward, our intrepid, patient, and thoughtful fellow traveler, went beyond the pale of expectations for an editor. We share with her our deepest thanks for journeying with us.

Laura would like to thank her family for all of their support, and especially her daughter, Cassy, for her patience and boundless energy. She will be part of the next generation to speak up for justice.

Stan thanks his husband, David Carroll, for his love and support.

In writing a book like this, we had to make choices about which details to include and which to leave out. We selected those aspects that felt most important in telling Fred's story in the most accurate and compelling way—but writing nonfiction always means finding our own version of the story. Any inaccuracies are our own.

❀ ❀ ❀

Heyday thanks the following donors for their generous contributions to this project:

Karen and Thomas Mulvaney

Suzanne Abel; Carrie Avery and Jon Tigar; Judy Avery; Lucinda Barnes; Jennifer Bates; Richard and Rickie Ann Baum; Sara Becker; Kate Black; Barbara Boucke; Barbara and John Boyle; John Briscoe; David and Pamela Bullen; Helen Cagampang; Bea Calo; Joanne Campbell; Dennis Carty; James and Margaret Chapin; David Chu; Cynthia Clarke; Raymond and Eva Cook; Roberta Cordero; Steve Costa and Kate Levinson; Robert Dawson and Ellen Manchester; Thomas Delebo and Bernie Feeney; Chris Desser and Kirk Marckwald; Lokelani Devone and Annette Brand; Michael Eaton and Charity Kenyon; Judith and Robert Flynn; Patrick Golden; Elizabeth Goldstein; Dr. Erica and Barry Goode; James Guerard; Kenji Hakuta and Nancy Goodban; Cricket Halsey; Francine Hartman and Chris De Marco; Anna Hawken; Nettie Hoge; Donna Ewald Huggins; Tom Killion; Susan Kirsch; Guy Lampard and Suzanne Badenhoop; Rebecca LeGates and Jonathan Root; Kerry and Dewey Livingston; David Loeb; Gary Malazian; Reuben Margolin and Amber Menzies; Kathy Martinez; Pamela Mendelsohn; Mary and Joe Morganti; Mark Murphy; Richard Nagler; Jean and Gary Pokorny; James and Caren Quay; Steven Rasmussen and Felicia Woytak; Kristine Reveles; Robin Ridder; Lennie and Mike Roberts; Alexandra Rome; Spreck Rosekrans and Isabella Salaverry; Peter Rosenwald; Becky Saeger and Tom Graves; Joanne Sakai and Dallas Foster; Peter Schrag and Patricia Ternahan Ttee; Toby and Sheila Schwartzburg; Mary Selkirk and Lee Ballance; Peter Selz and Carole Schemmerling; Jennifer Sime; Carla Soracco and Donna Fong; Linda Spencer; Kimberly Stevenot; Azile and Marcus White; and Al Young.

SOURCE NOTES

1. GETTING A HAIRCUT

Pages 1–2: "Hey boy...kind": Karen Korematsu in discussion with the coauthors, October 22, 2015.

2. PRUNING ROSES

Page 7: "How would you like to be called Fred?" Lorraine Bannai, *Enduring Conviction: Fred Korematsu and His Quest for Justice* (Seattle: University of Washington Press, 2015), 12.

5. DECIDING TO DEFY

Page 26: "Go ahead...You're old enough": *Of Civil Wrongs and Rights: The Fred Korematsu Story*, directed by Eric Paul Fournier (2000; New York: Docurama, 2007), DVD.

Page 27: "Jap this and Jap that": Fred Korematsu, unedited transcript, interview for *Of Civil Wrongs and Rights: The Fred Korematsu Story,* 20:04:10.

6. SAYING YES

Page 33: "You got a visitor": Fred Korematsu, unedited transcript, interview for *Of Civil Wrongs and Rights: The Fred Korematsu Story*, 20:38:05.

Page 33: "I would like to help you": Fred Korematsu, unedited transcript, interview for Of Civil *Wrongs and Rights: The Fred Korematsu Story*, 20:39:39.

Page 34: "We'll fight it...all the way": Fred Korematsu, interview by Lorraine Bannai and Tetsuden Kashima, May 14, 1996, Densho Visual History Collection, archive.densho.org/main.aspx.

7. LIVING IN A HORSE STALL

Page 40: "This was made for...better than this": Bannai, *Enduring Conviction*, 45.

Page 40: "Ma and Pa...come along:" Fred Korematsu, unedited transcript, interview for Of Ci*vil Wrongs and Rights: The Fred Korematsu Story*, 20:50:57.

Page 41: "Dumbell...such a thing?": Bannai, *Enduring Conviction*, 61.

8. FEELING LIKE AN ORPHAN

Page 48: "Just a little wind...made of cloth": Fred Korematsu to Ernest Besig, undated, Fred Korematsu Correspondence, American Civil Liberties Union of Northern California Records, California Historical Society, MS 3580, Box 56, Folder 1387.

Page 49: "I don't even know...like an orphan": Fred Korematsu to Ernest Besig, July 23, 1943, Fred Korematsu Correspondence, American Civil Liberties Union of Northern California Records, California Historical Society, MS 3580, Box 56, Folder ACLU 1386.

9. GETTING THE LETTER

Page 55: "I am very anxious to hear the outcome of our case": Fred Korematsu to Ernest Besig, March 3, 1943, Fred Korematsu Correspondence, American Civil Liberties Union of Northern California Records, California Historical Society, MS 3580, Box 56, Folder ACLU 1385.

Page 56: "Nice going": Fred Korematsu to Ernest Besig, undated, Fred Korematsu Correspondence, American Civil Liberties Union of Northern California Records, California Historical Society, MS 3580, Box 56, Folder ACLU 1385.

Page 57: "Am I an American or not?": Fred Korematsu, unedited transcript, interview for Of Civil *Wrongs and Rights: The Fred Korematsu Story*, 21:06:49.

10. REBUILDING, 1945 TO 1966

Page 63: "What's this about?": Karen Korematsu, interview by Lorraine Bannai and Tetsuden Kashima, May 14, 1996, Densho Visual History Collection, archive.densho.org/main.aspx.

Page 63: "Why didn't anybody tell me?": Karen Korematsu in conversation with coauthors, October 22, 2015.

Page 65: "We don't cut Jap hair": "Daniel Inouye: Returning to Prejudice," PBS, accessed February 22, 2016, www.pbs.org/thewar/detail_5281.htm.

11. UNCOVERING LIES, 1982

Page 70: "They did me a great wrong": Bannai, *Enduring Conviction*, 148.

Page 71: "Are you a…be my lawyer?": Peter Irons, interview by Alice Ito and Lorraine Bannai, October 27, 2000, Densho Visual History Collection, archive.densho.org/main.aspx.

Page 71: "Hey, these look…they're the best": Fred Korematsu, remarks at the conference "Judgments Judged and Wrongs Remembered: Examining the Japanese American Civil Liberties Cases of World War II on Their 60th Anniversary," Japanese American National Museum, Los Angeles, CA, November 5–6, 2004.

12. MAKING THE CASE, 1983

Pages 78–79: "Your Honor…race, creed, or color": Transcript, Motion to Vacate Conviction and Dismiss Indictment of Fred T. Korematsu, November 10, 1983, File 27635, Criminal Case Files, 1851–1982, US District Courts for the San Francisco Division of the Northern District of California, RG 21, records of the District Courts of the United States, NARA-SF, 30–32.acc.

Page 79: "Fred, you won. You won your case!": Dale Minami, interview by Tom Ikeda and Margaret Chon, February 8, 2003, Densho Visual History Collection, archive.densho.org/main.aspx.

Page 79: "That's good. That's really good": Dale Minami, interview by Tom Ikeda and Margaret Chon, February 8, 2003, Densho Visual History Collection, archive.densho.org/main.aspx.

Page 82: "It was a very brave thing that you did to stand up against the government": Bannai, 209.

Page 83: "You always have to…your rights": Bannai, *Enduring Conviction*, 199.

Page 84: "No one should ever be locked away…terrorist": Fred Korematsu, "Do We Really Need to Relearn the Lessons of Japanese American Internment?" *San Francisco Chronicle*, September 16, 2004.

BIBLIOGRAPHY

Books

Bannai, Lorraine. *Enduring Conviction: Fred Korematsu and His Quest for Justice.* Seattle: University of Washington Press, 2015.

Irons, Peter. *Justice at War: The Story of the Japanese American Internment Cases.* New York: Oxford University Press, 1983.

US Government Printing Office. *Personal Justice Denied: Report of the Commission on Wartime Relocation and Internment of Civilians.* 1982 and 1983. Reprint. Seattle: University of Washington Press, 1997.

Films

Of Civil Wrongs and Rights: The Fred Korematsu Story. Directed by Eric Paul Fournier. 2000. New York: Docurama, 2007. DVD.

Unfinished Business: The Japanese American Internment Cases. Directed by Steven Okazaki. 1984. Berkeley, CA: Farallon Films, 2005. DVD.

Online Resources

American Civil Liberties Union (ACLU): The ACLU works to defend and preserve the individual rights and liberties guaranteed by the Constitution and laws of the United States. www.aclu.org.

Densho: The Japanese American Legacy Project is a digital archive of videotaped interviews, photographs, documents, and other materials relating to the Japanese American experience. Densho is dedicated to preserving, educating, and sharing the story of World War II–era incarceration of Japanese Americans in order to deepen understandings of American history and inspire action for equity. www.densho.org.

Fred T. Korematsu Institute: Fred's daughter Karen Korematsu, founder and executive director, leads the Institute's mission of "Educating to Advance Racial Equity, Social Justice, and Human Rights for All." The Institute supports teachers to teach students about Fred's civil rights story, the World War II Japanese American incarceration, and, through public awareness, to inspire advocacy and civic engagement. www.korematsuinstitute.org.

IMAGE AND TEXT CREDITS AND PERMISSIONS

Heyday thanks the museums, public agencies, and private collections from which the images in this book were borrowed.

1. GETTING A HAIRCUT
Page 3: courtesy of Karen Korematsu at the Fred T. Korematsu Institute

Page 4: top: "The Irish Frankenstein," from *Punch*, May 20, 1882; bottom: "Pacific Chivalry," by Thomas Nast, *Harper's Weekly*, 1869, courtesy of the Bancroft Library, AP2.H3 v.13: 512

Page 5: top: © Elliott Erwitt/Magnum Photo; bottom: photo by Russell Lee, © Russell Lee Photograph Collection, ID e_rl_14646_0038, The Dolph Briscoe Center for American History, The University of Texas at Austin

2. PRUNING ROSES
Page 9: courtesy of Karen Korematsu at the Fred T. Korematsu Institute

Page 10: courtesy of Karen Korematsu at the Fred T. Korematsu Institute

Page 11: top: courtesy of the National Archives and Records Administration

Page 11: bottom: *Untitled* ("No Japs Wanted") by Henry Sugimoto, courtesy of the Japanese American National Museum, gift of Madeleine Sugimoto and Naomi Tagawa, 92.97

3. BEING A TEEN
Page 15: courtesy of Karen Korematsu at the Fred T. Korematsu Institute

Page 16: photo of Wong Kim Ark from 1904, courtesy of the National Archives and Records Administration (296479)

Page 17: top left: photo by William Warby, 2007, www.flickr.com/photos/wwarby; top right: courtesy of the California Historical Society, FN-18240; bottom: courtesy of the National Archives and Records Administration

4. EXPLODING, 1941
Page 21: top and bottom: Pearl Harbor, December 7, 1941, US Navy, courtesy of the National Archives and Records Administration

Page 22: top: courtesy of the *San Francisco Chronicle*; bottom: photo by Dorothea Lange, March 1942, courtesy of the National Archives and Records Administration (210-G-A35) via the Library of Congress

Page 23 (top): *My Papa* by Henry Sugimoto, courtesy of the Japanese American National Museum, gift of Madeleine Sugimoto and Naomi Tagawa, 92.97; bottom: courtesy of Brenda Wong Aoki and the Aoki Family Archive

5. DECIDING TO DEFY

Page 26: photo by Dorothea Lange, April 11, 1942, for the Department of the Interior, War Relocation Authority, courtesy of the National Archives and Records Administration (536017)

Page 29: left: courtesy of the National Archives and Records Administration (520053); right: courtesy of UCLA Charles E. Young Research Library Department of Special Collections, *Los Angeles Times Photographic Archives,* © Regents of the University of California, UCLA Library

Page 30: top: photo by Dorothea Lange, April 27, 1942, for the Department of the Interior, War Relocation Authority, courtesy of the National Archives and Records Administration (537745); middle: photo by Dorothea Lange, May 6, 1942, for the Department of the Interior, War Relocation Authority, courtesy of the National Archives and Records Administration (537889); bottom: *Junkshop Man Took Away Our Icebox* by Henry Sugimoto, courtesy of the Japanese American National Museum, gift of Madeleine Sugimoto and Naomi Tagawa, 92.97

Page 31: top: United States Army war propaganda poster, sourced from *Maximum Advantage in Pictures: Propaganda as Art and History*, chumpfish3.blogspot.com/2010/03 /this-is-enemy.html; bottom: "How to Spot a Jap," art by Milton Caniff, in *Pocket Guide to China* prepared by Special Service Division, Services of Supply, United States Army

6. SAYING YES

Page 36: top: courtesy of the American Civil Liberties Union of Northern California; bottom: students at Cypress Street School, courtesy of the Local History Collection, Orange Public Library, Orange, CA

Page 37: © by Toyo Miyatake

7. LIVING IN A HORSE STALL

Page 40–44: photos by Dorothea Lange for the Department of the Interior, War Relocation Authority, courtesy of the National Archives and Records Administration: page 40: April 29, 1942 (537670); page 43: top: April 27, 1942 (537480); bottom: April 29, 1942 (537675); page 44: top: June 16, 1942 (537894); bottom: April 29, 1942 (537677)

Page 45: drawing by Miné Okubo (community toilets, Tanforan Assembly Center, San Bruno, CA, 1942), courtesy of the Japanese American National Museum, gift of Miné Okubo Estate, 2007.62

8. FEELING LIKE AN ORPHAN

Page 48: Letter from Fred Korematsu to Ernest Besig, American Civil Liberties Union of Northern California Records, call number MS 3580, Box 56, Folder 1387, courtesy of the California Historical Society

Page 50: map by Ben Pease Cartography

Page 51: photo by Tom Parker, October 18, 1942, for the Department of the Interior, War Relocation Authority, courtesy of the National Archives and Records Administration (538677)

Page 52: drawing by Miné Okubo (dust storm at Easter service, Central Utah Relocation Project, Topaz, Utah, 1942–1944), courtesy of the Japanese American National Museum, gift of Miné Okubo Estate, 2007.62

Page 53: top: drawing by Chiura Obata, courtesy of the Obata family; bottom: photo by Grant Young, April 18, 2014, courtesy of USFWS Mountain-Prairie, https://www.flickr.com/photos/usfwsmtnprairie; poem by Kimii Nagata, reprinted by permission of the Nagata-Yamauchi Educational Fund (www.nyef.org)

9. GETTING THE LETTER

Page 57: Letter from Fred Korematsu to Ernest Besig, American Civil Liberties Union of Northern California Records, call number MS 3580, Box 56, Folder 1387, courtesy of the California Historical Society

Page 58: © Harris & Ewing, Collection of the Supreme Court of the United States

Page 59: left: "Exclusion Order Held Justified," December 18, 1944, courtesy of *The Bakersfield Californian*; right: Korematsu v. United States, 323 U.S. 214 (1944) at 219–222

10. REBUILDING, 1945–1966

Page 65: courtesy of the Daniel K. Inouye Institute

Page 66: courtesy of Karen Korematsu at the Fred. T. Korematsu Institute

Page 67: top: the March on Washington, August 28, 1963, for the United States Information Agency, courtesy of the Bureau of Public Affairs; bottom: California Grape Strike demonstration, 1965–1970, © United Farm Workers, courtesy of the Walter P. Reuther Library, Wayne State University (image ID 303)

11. UNCOVERING LIES, 1982

Page 73: top left: © Mario Gershom Reyes; top right: courtesy of Karen Korematsu at the Fred T. Korematsu Institute; bottom; memorandum, Edward Ennis to Herbert Wechsler, September 30, 1944, Box 1, Folder 3, Fred T. Korematsu v. United States *Coram Nobis* Litigation collection (Collection 545), courtesy of the UCLA Library Special Collections, Charles E. Young Research Library, UCLA

Page 74: courtesy of Nikkei for Civil Rights & Redress (formerly the National Coalition for Redress/Reparations), photo by Gann Matsuda

Page 75: courtesy of the Asian Law Caucus

12. MAKING THE CASE, 1983

Page 81: top: photo by Sibylla Herbrich, courtesy of the *Daily Journal*; bottom: photo by Shirley Nakao, courtesy of the Fred T. Korematsu Institute

Page 82: top: photo by Shirley Nakao, courtesy of the Fred T. Korematsu Institute; bottom: courtesy of Karen Korematsu at the Fred T. Korematsu Institute

Page 83: top: Civil Liberties Act of 1988, courtesy of the National Archives and Records Administration; bottom: photo by Jeffrey Bary, September 11, 2001, www.flickr.com/photos/70118259@N00/with/2847716157

Page 85: photo by Lia Chang, courtesy of the Fred T. Korematsu Institute

Page 89: courtesy of Karen Korematsu at the Fred T. Korematsu Institute

INDEX

Note: Numbers in **boldface** refer to illustrations.

ABOUT THE AUTHORS

photo: Jan Thyer

photo: Michael Woolsey

Laura Atkins is a children's book author and editor who grew up in an activist family and participated in social justice work herself, with a focus on diversity and equity in children's books. She lives in Berkeley, California, with her daughter and their dog. Find out more at www.lauraatkins.com.

Stan Yogi is coauthor, with Elaine Elinson, of *Wherever There's a Fight: How Runaway Slaves, Suffragists, Immigrants, Strikers, and Poets Shaped Civil Liberties in California.* For fourteen years he managed development programs at the ACLU of Northern California.

ABOUT THE ILLUSTRATOR

Yutaka Houlette is an illustrator and designer living in Oakland, California, with his wife and twin boys. He grew up in Japan and later moved to Baltimore to study art at the Maryland Institute College of Art. To see more of his work, visit yutakahoulette.com.